Hitchhikers to Eden

Hitchhikers to Eden

Poems by

Jean Biegun

Cover design by Shay Culligan
Cover image by Valeriia Miller

ISBN: 978-1-63980-184-8

Kelsay Books
502 South 1040 East, A-119
American Fork, Utah 84003
Kelsaybooks.com

For my children

Emily, Noah and Madeline,

my grandsons Justice and Theo,

and my great grandson Sekani

Acknowledgments

The author gratefully acknowledges the editors of the following publications in which these poems appeared previously, some in slightly different form.

Amethyst Review: "Sacred Numerology"
Ancient Paths Online: "Stations of Lent"
Ariel Chart: "Old Singers"
As It Ought to Be Magazine: "Hospice"
Eastern Iowa Review: "Green Bowl," 2021 Christine Prose Poetry Award
Fox Cry Review: "Signs & Wonders"
Free Verse (*Verse Wisconsin* since 2009): "Homespun"
Goose River Anthology: "Gulls in Wind," "Stations of Winter"
Great Lakes Calendar 2010–11 (Wisconsin Department of Natural Resources): "Autumn River"
Making It Speak: Poets and Artists in Cahoots (Sheboygan Visual Artists): "Crane Days"
Mobius: The Poetry Magazine: "Jazz Play"
Muddy River Poetry Review: "85 Candles at Shady Pines"
Mused: BellaOnline Literary Journal: "Mired in Blue"
Presence: International Journal of Spiritual Direction: "Heart of Job"
Red Eft Review: "The Wooden Urn with Carved Daisies"
Time of Singing: "Pastel Blue," "Spring Discovery"
Wisconsin Poets Calendar: "Leaving Yuma," "Spring Palette"

Contents

I.
Hitting the Road

Hospice

It's nothing I can talk about, June—
I don't even know how to be here.
I sat once with a friend who was giving
birth. That I could do, but you:
I can wash your floor, but I'm no good
at pushing you to heaven.

Let me try, though, June. Listen,
there are 16 hushed angels
at the edge of the bed, and listen,
June, they are hugging quite happily
and humming an ethereal anthem.

I'm not making any of this up.
Easter Bunny and Tooth Fairy
are here, too, as well as the winner
of the 6th Annual Spelling Contest
who crowned you the 7th. He passed
on in Viet Nam, 34 years ago this month,
remember?

He is kneeling here by your elbow
and grinning your favorite winning words—
grandeur and *halcyon.* How did you
know the letters in *halcyon* back then,
June, without knowing the definition:
tranquil?

I am counting 7 leprechauns all
with bunches of 4-leaf clovers ready
to stuff in your hands. It will be
a blast, I can see right now.

Gulls in Wind

I watched eleven gulls
face a hard wind.
All stood on the sand
at sober, crisp attention.
Some would quickstep
right or left and then as quickly
realign to the keen wind.
Others preened the sand
out of their feathers
when the gusts blew less.
In rough bursts, I saw
every bird hunker Sphinx-like
facing that fierce wind.
They seemed to know readily
what to do in the difficult moments.

More gulls joined the group
to total twenty-three,
but they scattered when a lone man
on lunch break strolled near.
He moved past, and four
returned to alert position
forward to the wind.
Others landed to join them.
I could tell they knew
what to do with tough times,
so I stayed in my car
in the lot at the beach
to watch them and to learn.

Homespun

I patch beat-down lines in poems
though most hold up rightly without
me. I sit inside their thin layers
too tired to stick my head out.

Oh, workaday verses, not tricky
nor starched . . . they do start truly
enough but leave me dwindled
and sad, like something that could be

isn't, like echoes in Orphan Annie's tune:
tomorrow, tomorrow. I come from women
who ate parts no one else grabbed—
necks, wings, gristle bits, apples wormed

and brown at their cores. I ball up
in dished-out casserole poems—compelled
but hopeful of sweet, distant outcomes.
I've waited so long for mangoes or a swell

vacation to a beach where flowered breezes
would sing me queen. I want a silver fast
dreamy jet to fly me to new lands and real pearl
buttons on my dresses and every seam to last.

Crane Days

Like winds and sunsets, wild
things were taken for granted
until progress began to do
away with them.
—Aldo Leopold, *Sand County Almanac*

Some days I just want
to take County B
and see open fields,

leave behind the city's center,
get on patched asphalt,
drive by a fallen-down barn.

The heart needs
leaping at tall tree lines,
swooning with blowing dune grass.

The eyes hold to wide horizons,
the thickly lived forest
and rambling riverways.

A flock of cranes rattles skyward.
One could wait in a wild place
for dusk forever
before turning back home.

Stations of Lent

I've been thinking about sin lately,
the push of black and white hats in the world.
Here at Supercuts waiting for a trim

I watch new piles of clippings
get swept up by Kori, my confessor this week.
She nods soft sympathy

while intuiting my crimes:
No, the kids won't be home for Easter . . .
too busy, new jobs and all.

My gray hairs fall on the cape around my neck,
DNA strands spiraled tightly in each snip,
sins of the father and mothers,

generations that still keep growing from my head.
Kori has blessed me with a clean look this time.
I pull my knit cap down to keep warm

and hurry to the Full Canteen next door
for coffee and another try for forgiveness
of flashbacks in black and white hats.

Sacred Numerology

My sister points at a passing van
with *Faith Technologies* printed on its side.
Make a good tattoo she comments and bets me
that 40 percent of folks under 40 get tattoos
these days.

She likes her Biblical numbers and preaches
to me on three fingers that 40 is holy—
for 40 years the Israelites wandered the wilderness,
for 40 days Jesus fasted and fought temptation,
for 40 nights Noah waited and watched it rain.

She's turning 70 soon. Nothing special
about 70, nothing prophetic or even
mandala-worthy.
Only the numerical answer to the problem
how many times must we forgive
the ones who did us wrong. 70 times 7
I remember from my Bible School days.

She kids she might get a tattoo for her birthday—
Faith Technologies in bold letters needled
on her back to testify, like the van,
that handy tools are inside
(and she gestures fist to chest)
for fixing her years of wear and tear.

Mired in Blue

I write *Mired in Blue* and you, my reader,
see a blue, maybe a vat of mixed blues
sloppy, blurred and thick. You think

I might be blue, a blue
poet. You imagine many possibilities
but then suddenly remember

the dragging, dense midnight shade
of your marriage's slow dying,
and that dark sky time your mother

murmured *I feel so blue* while she
waited in a two-bed hospital room
to hear a new doctor pronounce

the cancer word.
Mired in Blue: the title makes you
read on for clarification

of what the writer means,
perhaps a fading pastel still holding
to walls like those in your almost-gone

daughter's room, or a magical cerulean
that matches the eyes of a man
who strode confidently through

your office and your mind
last Wednesday exactly at 9:02.
You take so much from my blue mire.

Leaving Yuma

Leaving Yuma, stick to main roads.
Don't answer the hall phone
at Jade's Motel. Toss flashbacks
of some girl's easy whispers
behind in the rolling tumbleweed.
Be the cowboy and ramble.

Don't stroll lone and lanky
to a smoke-dimmed booth in a diner
next to a broke-down Greyhound bus
nor stare long at the stranger
wearing crimson lipstick and pink lace.
Don't let loose you're stopping at Jade's
up the street. Hit the fast highway
and go.

Skip those rutted trails of silence,
eyes turned mountain hard,
skin and then years burned dark as dirt.
Leave Yuma any other way.

'58 Fairlane (or The Long Sentence)

He gunned his pa's Ford past Dengle's Drive-In
and asked if I like small towns, and I told him
I guess but not the ones that gossip as I recalled
Aunt Violet tsk-tsking over Beverly Monskey
who got preggers before the party line ladies said
she should and with no shiny rock on that precious
ring finger, and he said he liked the under 900
population places where maybe you got just
a single slow-down sign to let you cruise by
the biscuits 'n gravy truck stop and the houses
with rubber tire gardens, and then I knew
we would not go steady long for I did not want
sixty years with a boy whose eyes got wide just
for tractor pull contests and hot deals on shotguns
and remembered only that I do not burn bacon
nor flush out ducks too soon at the blind.

Green Bowl

Loving is scary because it zooms. You are glued to a something, I think, and then you feel whenever whatever zips away the pain that is too much. Liking I can do. Liking is this bowl of a rich Chinese green not seen anywhere in the slick city. Liking is enough sometimes but not really. I mean, the fabulous, fantastic stuff my roommate carefully cooks every evening, and with it we sip good merlot or a white. Wanting, if maybe I want a thing, do I love it? Is the thread of desire I send to it something? I love [*blank*]. I refuse to think of that which wants to be wrapped in my spinning web mind. After all, freedom comes in letting go (my mother's old hippie posters taught me) and don't we want to be free?

Tree in Union Park

A wounded tree in the park stopped me
tall though leaning a bit
thin bark strips flapping
a girth too narrow to claim much history

Lightning must have split several branches
that city workers then sawed off

Lacking a symmetry
yet lifting its few remaining limbs
the tree seemed to whistle in the spring breeze

I noticed the base was gashed on one side
while the crown mostly bare
showed life in a few green patches

With my own years I touched it
that naked instructor
unintentional sage

Heart of Job

It is important to say thank you
to the ground.
There is required bowing
and the necessary lowering
of every inner voice and veil.
Each day, each moment,
in supermarkets and car repair shops,
in a high school office
where the principal stares at forms,
the ground must be touched and thank-you
spilled over it
like proffered gold.

Somehow you have to hold them in your heart:
the hard stones caught in the craw
as well as the pretty blue gems you cradle.
And then you have to let them go,
release, spit all of it out,
let loose every gripped thing.
This is the only way, the way of Job,
the gladsome emptying out
of the heart and craw of Job.

II.
Almost There

Spring Discovery

Found a Lewis and Clark nickel in the coin jar
Last week, never had seen one before

Its decorated scenic back caught my eye
Like the shiny state quarters grandkids save

I squinted at the tiny inscription
And the pace of another cluttered day stopped

> *Ocean in view!*
> *O! The joy!*

The coin a sudden compass, talisman
Holy medal centering now in my pocket

Directing daily responsive readings
Spring discoveries

> *Returned blue heron in view!*
> *O! The joy!*

> *Shy new trillium in view!*
> *O! The joy!*

> *Blossoming dune in view!*
> *O! The joy!*

> *The joy!*

Pastel Blue

Like sap logs on fire, poems must sizzle
they tell me . . . *Make them tingle, burst out clever,*
surprising in the final line

But wanting only to linger by this cool
passable stream, I stick-write in soft clay
elementary phrases

No dancing in long stanzas flaring one way
then that, nor sassy crimson rhythms
for faded souls

Merely *Love you* . . . deep-grooved letters
in green-gray mud, a red-eyed vireo scolding near,
and me resolute in a fresh ironed dress,
my new one just sewn in pastel blue

Spring Palette

I've been painting my child's gaze,
searching for amber in cinnamon

brown lashes, harmonizing gladly
four blues and two golds in the sky

around his head. I lean toward
the canvas, consider pressing divinity

in the soft fold of cheek and mouth,
try to mix color like Raphael

himself transfixed by visions
of the Virgin and her Child.

Now I pose my own son's tendrils
darker than forest umber, richer

than that glimpse we caught on the hill
of a hawk's crimson tail feathers,

more vital than those meadowlarks
fresh at our feeder insistent on spring.

Stations of Winter

Here I finish these warmed
leftover beans and feel your
sharp focus on dark County J
where deer always cross.

Here I pause for this robin's egg
soft-blue old bowl and am pleased
we found the whole 30-piece set
under 19 bucks in Grall's antique store.

Here I catch our brave furnace tick
harder than faith itself to coax up
a welcome for you and the kids.

Here I turn on lights while winter's gray
kneels quietly by each window's chill.

Here I wait among photos and shadows
and indoor gleanings and strain
toward the voices I am bound to.

The Wooden Urn with Carved Daisies

Mother began as a tidy person,
hair primped just so for Sundays,
neck scarves tied according to photos
in her high school Home Ec book.

She'd rip out every crooked seam
we sewed on the treadle Singer,
scrubbed our hair three times with kerosene
when we brought home nits,
ironed even the sheets though the wind
flattened them pretty well on the line.

The day young Mel left for Viet Nam,
she washed every window including the cupola,
the high-up little room we never went to:
always told us cleaning something
was the start to fixing everything.

When he came back in a casket,
she let the flower beds go first,
and the daisies spread out helter-skelter.

Took years before her vegetable rows
came back somewhat straight,
for her skirt pleats to be almost crisp.
It was like mud had won out.

While the tumor did its slow dance
(*borderline* the word during that long turn),
she'd go to the garden,
sit on her short stool and sift the loosened
soil through her fingers.
No gloves.

Said she like the warmth of it,
the way it anchored everything,
trees and houses and people:
that it was what we lived on.
She laughed every time we pointed out
the dirt under her nails.

Old Singers

Old singers lounge in grooves
on dark vinyl   swoon to the high
notes   hold back their rasp

They imagine birds
dancing on sheet music   dream
in downbeat and gin

follow the smoke fog   sway
in cool clubs   romantic blue
they remember

They nod to the horn   smooth their
hips and tap time   while sugar
ivories smile

85 Candles at Shady Pines

Most days he will wake with his
marbles scattered—swirling balls
of worry and flummoxed puzzlement.

He will shuffle through a maze
of toddling walkers and canes
with handles carved like sleek horses.

Beeping scooters, then fumes of Pine-Sol
will lead him along beige halls to the tan
casseroles and Sinatra songs mapping
the dining room.

But on his magical clear-eye marble
days, he will grip that lucky shooter
with sure knuckles and knock all haze
out of play.

Those times he is hepcat ready for a
slick game, one more high-stepping day.

Jazz Play

Jazz croons every buck from your pocket
deals out sorghum laced with black flame
dares you play it back neat

Jazz gets drumsticks jamming like Picasso
bass lines dancing like Pollock flicked paint
solo tenor keening colors most can't dig

Mailman slides four past-due bills under the door
Corinne wants some new high-heel shoes
and all what else you brought home

Lucky riff of cobalt blows in the window
your fingers flex unconsciously
complex undertows in your belly laugh

One quick grab for your horn
J. D.'s keyboard smokes the blue air
and Mae's twins cook gumbo on strings and drum

Jazz is the harbor burning
with your boat anchored there
hot foam blinding above and sweet sirens below

No player rows to the pale side of the moon
over a sleeping summer bay
who has ever touched jazz heat

Only gamblers speed to that wail
search currents like screeching birds
dive for gold that can flash past your eyes

Signs & Wonders

For centuries, it was assumed that the snake she used
was an asp, but it is now thought the snake was an
Egyptian cobra.
                    —*Writer's Almanac,* August 30, 2005

The opinion now per *Writer's Almanac* is that Cleopatra
killed herself with an Egyptian cobra, not asp.
Did you know this was a hot issue in certain camps:

Naja haje versus *Vipera aspis?* I mean, couldn't whoever
snuck the snake into the Queen's guarded chamber
or spotted it angling off note details, tell some artist friend

who'd then paint the right reptile on a couple vases or wall?
I want evidence, don't you? It must have got away unseen.
Snakes are geniuses at escaping, and *where* evil Octavian

kept Cleo under wraps before his glitzy conqueror's march
past her woebegone buddies clearly was not *un*impregnable.
She'd managed to have the venomy weapon smuggled in.

My ex kept snakes. Did I tell you I stepped on one
that had shoved its tank lid off in the midst of a steamy
August night? Zounds, up to the couch leapt I!

How could she do it, let the fangy critter bite her? Did she
prod the cobra (not asp!) to rile it? I wish she'd kept a journal.
Do you understand her way to go? They were big on snakes,

those Egyptians, especially re their cobras: symbols. You
and I—we too let bites of life hinge on symbols. I depend
on that: your referencing me through back-pocket photos,

my rose petal cologne, pinches of cardamom in that soup
we claim ours at the corner restaurant, coded nudges, singing
overheard while raking the yard, and further conquests of heart.

Migration

I.

We from separate strains,
flight patterns taut and parallel
echoed congruent glaciers
ignorant lobes snowbound

We ground all before and within
to bedrock

As these we moved and failed
melted
finally melted
loosing every cold crevasse

II.

A hesitant chrysalis
this emergence of you and me

Instinct waiving gravity
we learn to follow the lift of air

Like whooping cranes flagging toward warmth
flailing past broke and dragged terrains
we try
for a butterfly solstice

Self-Portrait in Later Life

I don't know why
but it would start
with popsicle sticks—
that doesn't seem sensible or right
but it is the instinctive beginning

Glued to a surface
stick on stick rising
giving prominence to some features
a cleft here
a pronouncement there
so sun catches and warms
the built-up declarative facets

A triple-thick brow able
to withstand a low branch perhaps
or sudden fall
and a mouth confluencing
several sticks horizontally
into a wide grin
lips almost split with joy

And a vertical neck
long and held high
like Modigliani's women
though here the chin
tilted up
now up

Autumn River

You must give to the rivers
the kindness you would give
to any brother.
              —Chief Seattle

Autumn kayak takes you
close to sister wind.
Her quick laughter
lifts you near drying reeds,
by red-wing blackbird's
abandoned nests
quiet now these chilled days.

One hand in cold water
finds the marsh ready
for the season of rest.
Fat muskrat in cattails
sets to den-building.
You nod and paddle on.

Trees of yellowed leaves signal
to yield for a fallen branch.
This artery of water feels alive
around your thin floating shell.
You coast like a seed pod
trusting brother river, and
sister wind brings you home.

About the Author

Jean Biegun discovered the power and joy of poetry in a magical creative writing course in the century-turning year 2000. [*Thank you, Prof. Bruce Gans.*] After a career in special education with the Chicago Public Schools, she retired to rural Wisconsin. There in the town of Two Rivers, she wrote nature poems for Woodland Dunes Nature Center's seasonal newsletter for many years and published the chapbook *Waking Up at Woodland Dunes* in support of the preserve. Now living in California, she appreciates having found thriving communities of poets across the country from large cities and farm regions to university towns.